letters

POSTMARKED

from the

garden

Letters Postmarked From The Garden

Printed in association with Kindle Direct Publishing/CreateSpace, Charleston, SC.

Unless otherwise noted, Scripture quotations designated NKJV are from New King James Version.
ISBN: 9780692193785
Made in USA

Cover design: Melissa Shultz-Jones
Graphic design and design compilation: John Coburn
Layout and formatting: Katie Woods
Photography: Lily White Photography

POETRY **by**: Lisa Ann

Contents

Letters About Home

One Day .... Page 14
Even On My Best Days .... Page 15
Sing .... Page 16
Nowhere .... Page 17
Always .... Page 18
Battle Cry .... Page 19

Letters To Nostalgia And Left-Hand Turns

Thanksgiving .... Page 22
Bet On The 7 .... Page 23
To Grandmother's House .... Page 24
Just Let Go Already .... Page 26
Hello .... Page 27
Just Sweep It Under The Rug .... Page 28
The Little Girl On The Brick Wall .... Page 29
Lucky .... Page 33
September 30: Present Day .... Page 35
One Last Letter .... Page 36

Letters From The Ex Files

Thief .... Page 40
Things You Can Keep .... Page 41
To My First Forever .... Page 43
The Luggage I Should Have Left In California ... Page 45
First Day Of Grief .... Page 46

Blonde Hair, Blue Eyes, Black Soul   Page 47
Rings And Things   Page 50
To His Next Victim   Page 51
Better Without You   Page 53
Three Things   Page 54
Marriage Is...   Page 56
Satisfying The Unsatisfied   Page 59
Thoughts From Aisle 7   Page 62
I Always Knew   Page 63
The Reasons I Left You   Page 64
100% Cotton   Page 65
The Ex Files   Page 67

Letters From The Rosie Chronicles

To The Abuse Survivor   Page 70
We Should Write A Song Together   Page 72
But We Can't Go Back   Page 73
Moving Forward   Page 74
Time Heals   Page 76
The Aftermath   Page 77
Hush   Page 79
Appetizers   Page 80
Looks Aren't Everything   Page 81
Row For One, Please   Page 82
Revealed   Page 83

Letters About Dragons

Splattered Ink   Page 86
Due North   Page 87
Ebony   Page 88
Letters About Dragons   Page 89

Not My Battle   Page 91
Bitter Friendships   Page 92

Letters Of Sweet Nothings

Filters   Page 94
To My Favorite Tree   Page 95
Wake Up   Page 96
Discoveries   Page 97
Paper Love Story   Page 98
Investments   Page 99
Death   Page 100
Counting It All As Joy   Page 101
Dear Local Bookstore   Page 103

Letters To L.A.

Things I Know To Be True   Page 106
Wondering   Page 107
Daisies   Page 108
Because Enough Of My Past Life Was Spent In   Page 109
"Doing As The Gentiles"
Don't Send Me Flowers   Page 110
When Emotions Are Your Super Power   Page 112
Persistence   Page 113
To God Be The Glory   Page 114
Expectations   Page 115
Pillows And Promises   Page 116
True Story   Page 117
No One Is An Island   Page 118
Anxiety   Page 119
My Cup Overflows   Page 120
The Love Letter: Part I   Page 122

Until Now   Page 125
A Friendly Reminder   Page 128
The Love Letter: Part II   Page 130

Letters To Sidekicks

Paul   Page 134
Andy   Page 135
The Return   Page 136
To My Baby Sister's Babies   Page 138
Your Season   Page 140
Mikey   Page 141
Loida: My Forever Friend   Page 143
To My Favorite Katie   Page 144
Trace   Page 145
Davis: Welcome To The Book Club   Page 146
Curly Top   Page 147
Rhett   Page 148
Realization   Page 149

Letters To Strangers

Til' The Beginning   Page 152
The Social Butterfly   Page 153
Wonderfully Made   Page 154
Cleansing The Soul   Page 155

Letters To Codependents

What Remains   Page 158
Normal   Page 159
But You Knew That Already   Page 160
And They All Fall Down   Page 161

You Can't Blame The Boy   Page 162
Love Doesn't Fix Selfishness   Page 163
The Ripple Effect   Page 164

Letters To God

A Seal Of Our Union   Page 168
A.C.T.S.   Page 169
A Place To Call Home   Page 170
Underserving   Page 171
Ephesians 5:2   Page 172
Until You Do   Page 173
When It's Not Okay   Page 174
Home   Page 175
Lord's Supper Thoughts   Page 176
The Lord's Supper   Page 177
During The First Day Of The Week   Page 178
Joy   Page 179
Isaiah 53   Page 180
Promises   Page 181
Overcome   Page 182
My Kind Of Love   Page 183
New Words   Page 184
Longing   Page 185
Lisa's Song   Page 186
Even Still   Page 188

Letters To Maybe, One Day

Percentages   Page 190
As Dreamers Do   Page 191
To Neverland   Page 192
Passports   Page 193

One Day   Page 194
Ya See, It's Like This   Page 195
The Existence Of Love (Or Lack Thereof)   Page 197
Translation When I Say "You Are Not My Type"   Page 198
Verbs   Page 199
Choice   Page 201

Letters To Midnight Moon

Midnight Moon   Page 204
Fireflies   Page 205
False Promises   Page 206
To Remember No More   Page 207
Late Night Walks   Page 209
My Friend, The Moon   Page 210
A.D.D.   Page 211
Good Morning Sunshine, Good Night Moonlight   Page 212

Just One More Thing

P.S.   Page 215

The End

Acknowledgements   Page 219

Introduction

A passion for words has always been inside of me. I say always, but there was a time in my life that I lost my relationship with words. They had left me in my times of "fiery trials" (1 Peter 4:12). But then, in 2013, I found them again. For the first time in many years, I began writing.

In 2015, I decided to share my story with the world (and Amazon.com) with my mini book "The Stereotypical Dramatic Life of a Flower." I felt as though I had something to say and was driven by the idea that if it helped even just one person, it would be worth the effort.

In the years that followed, I discovered that my story was not over and there was more to be told. I find such strength and beauty from the idea that my story might be like yours and that, together, we can be confident that we are chosen and precious to God; and that in this, we can find healing, hope, love, and most of all, GOD.

And with that, I want to share with you these letters from my heart...

Lisa Ann

letters

—ABOUT—

home

One Day

One day I am going to belong —
Belong in a place that I have been waiting for
and think of as often as I breathe
Where we are all the same,
And we all love,
And we all see our Maker face to face.

Even On My Best Days

I still long for Heaven.

Sing

Sing through the tears,
Belt it out until there is nothing left but dry eyes
and your heart in His hands.
His promises will be what brings you through.

In listening to "Lights Will Guide You Home."

Nowhere

Without Him, I would have no hope
and nowhere to call

Home.

Always

Oh, how I look forward to the place where
there are no "Goodbyes."

Where there are no empty spaces in my heart.

And no broken promises.

No hurt and no water that swell up from the eyes.
Where I will forever gaze upon Christ's face.

Where I will bow at His feet.

Where I will sing and never grow tired.

Where every day is not only new, but also good.
No shadows. No darkness. No fear.

Always love. Always light.

Always home.

Battle Cry

The sun will shine in the dark
and the stars will lead us home.

And bravery happens when we smile for the sake of others
even though our heart hurts.

I cry out to God that my heart is heavy,
and I can't carry it alone.

I plead to my Heavenly Father to take my hand
and guide me to the place where there is no night.

And where I will once again see my friends
who never gave up the battle.

letters

To
Nostalgia
& Left-Hand
turns

Thanksgiving

The twists and turns I can make with my eyes closed.
I hear my Mother's voice as I signal right tell me,
"The driveway is not a raceway."

I still veer to the left, so as to avoid the pothole
in the crack-cemented way that used to be home.

Ancient trees filled with ticks
and memories of a child so young.
The rooms seem smaller — unfamiliar yet remembered.

Surrounded by yellow-stained walls
happily hearing children run in the halls—
children that hilariously just might be the worst
hide-n-seekers I have ever met.

We all sit in separate rooms now.
The television set stays on 24/7.

The TV set that raised me—
The Lazy-Boy that was my friend.
I am glad I came, but I must be going.

Bet On The 7

Things are just things.
We will soon rummage through an old house
that used to be called home.

We will clean it for the last time—
And things will be passed or claimed
that we will each grab onto that remind us
that you were once here.

And we cling to them like it's our last breath of air

Like holding on to these things will somehow bring you back.

And I know things are just things,
but for now, I will see these things and think of you,

and know, even though our time together
was never enough time,
I am thankful for them all the same.

To Grandmother's House

I close my eyes and envision myself step out of my car
and walk down a steep-hilled sidewalk
that had long ago kissed my knees more times than I wanted.

In my mind I can hear
the screen door of my grandmother's house make its
screeching noise

and I am transported to the house I grew up in

and it's safe;

with its shag brown carpet
and flower-patterned wallpaper,

and it's home.

As I sit on a blanket-covered couch
I hear the vinyl records she plays
and it is as if the music had never stopped.

I see my grandmother in the kitchen so clearly
as if I never needed glasses.

She is sassy and strong—
all the things I would later become

as if to make her legacy live on
and the thought of this makes a smile appear across my face.

So, as I shut the front door for the last time;

as I let the squeaky screen door slam,

still feeling the presence of her cringed anger come upon me
because I apparently never learned
to gently close doors as she liked

I leave comforted knowing this place will always stay alive
in my mind.

Just Let Go Already

The silent walls we have built around our relationship.

I have found myself screaming from the other side,
brick and mortar deafening the noise to a dull roar
that is like the humming sound of a VCR.

And we have become just that.

The hum of a VCR filled with ribbon of apathy and bitterness.

Twisting the rods to try to get back what we once had.

Sadly enough,
no one has those overweight pieces of machinery anymore,

and what we have become is numb plastic,
and something that cannot start over.

Hello

I took some books off the shelf tonight,
as if I had time to read anything at all.

I enjoy the feel of a good book,
the soft yellowed pages on my fingertips.

As I turned the pages of yet another book I will never finish,

your obituary fell out of it.

Maybe that's how we have always been;
Too busy to say anything else, but "hello."

Just Sweep It Under The Rug

I feel as though the grudges that we hold turn into clouds—
Translucent at first, but time turns them dark—
Like the smog check that will never pass inspection—

The dark clouds fogged our way to see the truth
to who we all are,
messy humans who so desperately need
to learn to give grace to each other
as Christ does for us,
and lean upon each other for comfort, as a family should.

We fell short in more than one regard to this.

So, the clouds eventually fell, and turned into dust,
that were just swept under the rug.

How disheartening it is to see what decades took to build,
took only one person's death to break apart.

The Little Girl On The Brick Wall

3:15 pm
I say goodbye to my classmates
as their parents pick them up.

I roam the halls.

3:45 pm
A wall of glass doors is on my right.

I sit Indian-style in a long blue and green-patterned
skirt on the brick wall aligning the flowerbed.

White button-down shirt with an embroidered symbol
on my left breast pocket.

4:00 pm
I sit here and act like this is normal.

I have learned how to hide behind the smiles.

I am too young to know this.

4:15 pm
The leaves are falling.

Colors of autumn surround me.

I never take my backpack off.

He will be here any minute.

4:30 pm
The band kids finish with practice.

They walk out of the glass doors to my right with confidence
as their parents wait on them in their minivans and
soccer mom SUVs.

5:00 pm
He lives only 10 minutes away.

He works from home.

It will be any minute now—I think.

5:15 pm
I could have gotten Mom to pick me up,
but I want to see him—

I long to see him.

5:25 pm
Any minute now.

5:30 pm
I see him as he pulls up.

I smile.

The wait was worth all of the embarrassing looks
I had received before.

5:31 pm
I open the door as he says,
"Hey Sweetie."
And at that moment I am okay.

I am 14 years old.

This is the moment that will shape my life without my consent.

This moment is a continuing, pathetic, desperate hope
in the life of a little girl who longs for the love
that her father should give.

Everyone has some type of moment in their life
that shapes them.

This was mine.

Lucky

I heard a poet once say about her own father,
"How dare you die on me?
How am I supposed to get this anger out now?"

For me, I guess the only way is to write it in a letter.

Dear Dad,

Lucky for you, I decided to marry men that were just like you,
and now I've learned to despise last names—
loathe them even.
And look at them as though they are merely
time-stamped lettering.

I had allowed your legacy to live on by falling in love with men
who only pretended to love me back and just like that
I became that little girl on the brick wall again—alone,
waiting on someone who didn't care about me,
yet always longing for him to.

I'm done with men like you.
Yes, you may have been sober that last year of your life on
this earth, but you ruined lives during your wake,

and those years took more time and more heartache
that might never go away.

People ask me,
"How can you love someone who doesn't care for you?"
I tell them, "It's easy. I learned as a child."

And I didn't know any different until now.

September 30: Present Day

His sin consumed him,

drinking debauchery like it was the last drop of any flavor
he would ever taste on his tongue.

I will do everything in my power to not let your legacy live on
in me or anyone else you never really loved.

Fifteen years later and I am still angry.

One Last Letter

Dear Dad,

This will be the last letter for a while.

When I was 19, I gave your eulogy.

I remember showing Mom what I wrote, and she made edits
that I hated because it turned into something different,
but I said it in edited form to simply appease.

I didn't know what to do in a eulogy,
so, I performed my first spoken word poem.

Today, I called Mom and said,
"Tell me something good about Dad."
I started feeling bad about being so angry with you.

I don't want every poem I write about you to only be of my
anger towards you.

I want to let others know you had good qualities, too.

I remember us staying up late and watching TV,
reclined on the Lazy-Boy until we passed out.

I remember you embarrassing me when I got my period by bringing home a dozen roses, handing them to me and saying, "Now you're a woman."

I remember your greatest gift was always
making me laugh,
no matter how I felt.
When you would speak, laughter would soon follow.

I know I got my sarcasm from you.

I believe it to be one of my greatest traits.

(Everyone thinks so, too.)

So, today, I called Mom, and she told me that from the moment I learned to walk,
wherever you went, I would follow you.

So, you see, I have always loved you.
I still do.

The question that remains is, "Why didn't you?"

letters FROM THE EX-FILES

Thief

I had a dream about him the other night.
I guess I always try to go back to what is familiar.

But he was never good, and I will always have him
frozen in my mind as the boy who took away forever.

Things You Can Keep

I saw you again for the first time in a decade—
through the pixelated portal of social media.

I didn't search for you—

I was content on never seeing you again, but it happened.

And when it happened those all too familiar feelings
came back.

Though not as intense, they came back all the same
rushing over me like a warm fire.

It wasn't those silly butterflies or lightheaded happiness;
It was the pain in my chest, right where life flows—

And it hurt.

But I prayed that I never forget,
those scars that can reveal themselves at any time
might pain me, but the pain will not linger long.

And I prayed that I find purpose in the pain.
And although the scars will forever be,

light will shine through and give healing.

And although you will forever be the boy who broke my heart
and made me cry;

my love for you—that I gave to you—
will not be asked to be given back.

To My First Forever

When I look into your father's eyes,
I see you,
and what you could have become.

His eyes twinkle and I imagine your smile.
But when I see these new lines in the corners of his eyes
I am reminded of the late nights you have caused him—
And your mother.

I wish I could tell them how they do not
bear this burden alone.

I never gave up on us—
You just gave me no choice but to leave.

You were my first forever, probably my last.

How sad that I now see my first forever as
a bittersweet tragedy,
but if I took off the rose-tinted glasses I would see it
for what it was: a train wreck.

Funny, how time can be deceptive like that,

making me think of our love as these young kids
oblivious to life;
young and carefree,
but foolish with blindfolds on to who we were together.

But, you will never read this letter.
And in the same way we said "Goodbye"
we will never again say,
"Hello."

The Luggage I Should Have Left In California

I feel as though I am constantly running from him,
As if he is lurking behind the trees,
or, because he has no shame,
Appears in the noon of day—
All this because he still exists.

My nightmares last a long time
as I fight to get rid of him,
as he still lurks in the shadows,
behind the trees, in the noon of day.

If I realize the reality of him—
That he is just a sad, twisted, disgusting,
worthless piece of human flesh.

He chose to be this,
I write it all down, say it out loud,
as to make him appear small, not human, not good,
because he isn't.

Because he chose to be this way,
unashamed,
lurking behind the trees in the noon of day.

First Day Of Grief

I am just now grieving us.

The "us" that, if it still existed,
could now be counted on all fingers,
starting on toes,
counting to the forever that was stolen by

an artificial,
L'Oreal-bottled blonde.

I never got to say "Goodbye" to you
and the toxicity of a marriage
that burned overnight like a poorly lit campfire.

I was too preoccupied with my ship and sail,
I never bothered to look back
at the boy standing on the pier
with his middle finger in the air—

Never said "Goodbye" or asked the boy
if he really meant "forever" and all the "I love yous."

Instead, I wrapped those questions with a bow
colored in adultery as my answer.

Blonde Hair, Blue Eyes, Black Soul

When he would abuse me,

I would lock myself in a room that could not protect me,
still closed out from the world with no windows for escape.
Only the grip of his apathetic arms waiting for me
to open the door.

When I discovered he cheated on me
over, and over, and over again,
I was still scared to go out in the world,
so instead I hid in the closet.

Those rooms where we once sat, lay, or where I cried...
those rooms seemed to have no oxygen.
I slept in the closet, being comforted now
by a place of nothingness, which is what I was at the time.

And when I also discovered that I didn't fulfill his sexual needs
by letting him rape me,
and empty me
little by little each time
I became even more numb and hollow—

I was like a tree cut down to a stump.

All of my branches, my leaves, my fullness
had been tossed into a factory of used goods.

And when I discovered that his adulterous actions were with
prostitutes—as if anyone knew those still existed—
and as he placed himself into each of them,
he broke the oneness that we had once
vowed to God to keep.

As if he weren't killing me each time he touched me.

He finally became a tyrant in my eyes—
the tyrant he always was.

When he told me his thoughts on marriage,
that if he got married, it would "fix" his "problem"—
as if I were an experiment,
a case study to be tried, tortured, and tweaked
to his specifications,
to make him cured of his disease.

But the trial of this case study on this unwilling participant
ended with notarized papers and a woman that would never
be experimented on again.

I guess there should be an ending to this poem—
I never want to leave without giving a ray of hope,
so here it is...

I was released from the bondage of a tarnished,
broken soul.

And although I am left with the aftermath
of becoming used goods,
I remind myself that the new craze is to recycle
and that I am a woman that refused to sink
and be choked out by an already broken man.

Rings And Things

You have given your soul to Satan
on a silver platter.

And he melted that platter into a ring
by which to control you.

To His Next Victim

He will tell you that you are his world—
and you will believe his deceptive innocence.

You will waste countless breaths
and minutes upon years
waiting for him to love you like you dreamed.

Like he said he did.
Go ahead and exhale because that day will not arrive.

He will have you to believe you are crazy—
that it isn't abuse—
that he never cheated—
that it wasn't rape—
that he was sorry—

Please, when this happens,
and it will,
realize that he was broken long before
he ever met either of us.

You will start to tell yourself that you are trapped.
Accept what fate has placed in your lap...
That it is your lot in life—

This is when you need to run because
the numbness is starting to take hold of your entire being.

If you are anything like me,
and I assume you are because he likes his victims the same—
naïve, kind, and beautiful—
and like the wind, he took you away.

And like the night, you never saw in the dark
the gnashing of his teeth and his darts fly at your heart.

And again, if you are anything like me,
you will not believe the warning signs
because you still see the good in people.

And again, he will tell you that he loves you.
He will tell you to fall into his arms
and when you finally pick yourself up from the rubble
with scratched knees and jagged edges,
grab some Band-Aids, open the door, and never look back.

And when he moves on from you, only then
will you understand why you never received this letter.
Because we both know there will always be another victim.

Better Without You

I went through all the "what ifs" in my mind,
and I realized that I would not have liked the person
I would have become with you
because I would not have become who I am now.

Three Things

I am not a hoarder.
My attic consists only of dust, spider webs, a Mac box
and a notebook that I never look at.

I see things as dust collectors, so I keep very little.
But the ones I keep in a box
hidden from the sunlight are few.

One.
A Nokia phone with a yellow screen,
the game snake, and a cheap plastic cover.
This phone is well over a decade old.
I keep it because of the words that are on it.

When I turn the phone on,
 I read this simple text message from my father,
"How you doin'?"

It reminds me that he once breathed with me on this earth.

Two.
A poem.
A cheesy love poem full of rhymes and empty promises
from my ex-husband.

54

It reminds me that for a moment,
I thought he could love someone more than himself.

Three.
A chip.
A round chip with the number 30 on it.
This chip reminds me that from a five-year relationship,
that someone cared,
someone tried for 30 days.

It's a box filled with nothings from people of my past
who quit trying.

I keep these things like the dried flowers
we keep from funerals of our loved ones.

This is all I have left of them,
these are their funeral flowers.

The death of people who were never really mine.

Marriage Is...

Marriage is month of bliss.

It is having a slumber party every night with your best friend,
who happens to be the opposite sex.
A best friend who you can make out with.

It is having someone to talk with, have adventures with,
and be content with playing scrabble on New Year's Eve with.

Fast forward...

Marriage is years of sadness.

A bed with pillows, blankets, you, and your dog.

It is to control you.

It is to ask of you your entire life physically,
while trying to break your soul.

It is his fake tears saying,
"I'm sorry," immediately after it has been done.

It is your precious tears behind the smiles.

It is the exhaustion of refusing to give up hope while
you are screaming inside and keeping composure outside.

It turns men into tyrants.

It unleashes the beast, and what you thought was love was
merely the devil playing a cruel joke on your heart.

You are the canvas that is now painted black
with rips in the worn fabric that can never be patched.

It is innocence lost and broken dreams.
It is never looking at a man—any man—all men
the same again.

In the beginning, marriage makes you feel like a princess.
Soon, you will learn the reality:
that Cinderella was a naïve dreamer
with shards of glass in her feet.

It is invisible bruises on your mind, heart, and body
that you get,

and suddenly you are struck with OCD—
trying to wash them away in a scalding hot shower.

It is love that was never returned.

It is a love that left you with memories of broken glass
and a certificate that is too sad to frame.

Satisfying The Unsatisfied

He tells me that I have potential.

I cling to it like the last strand of rope
on a mountain I could never climb.

He tells me that he is sorry.
I hold on to those words with bitterness and tears,
as I lock myself in a room that won't protect me.

He tells me that he doesn't know how he paid for it.
I am repulsed at his irrevocable lie
that spits out of his adulterous mouth.

He tells me that he abused me because
his religion said he could.

It was in these words that I realized what he was.

He tells me that I'm lovable.

The words he gives me when I sit and wonder
why he never did.

Then I broke through.

I finally struck a chord on an instrument
that has long been rusted and dead
when he raged at my actions of bringing up his past.

He shouts in frustration when I wanted to know
if he abused her the way he did me.
These are the words I hold on to.

It was at that moment, when I played my most delicate chord.
It sang to me, and for once I exhaled.

From the countless days—
over 1,800 days' worth of lies—
I got one day.

More like five minutes.
But those five minutes will stay with me
more than the thousands.

Confession. Just one.

That one breath was like coming up for air
after what seemed to be a lifetime underwater.

This is just a small portion of a day in the life of living with a narcissist.

Being codependent on a drug that will make you go insane, unless you realize that there is no satisfying the unsatisfied.

I will say to God, my Rock,
"Why have You forgotten me?
Why do I go mourning because of the oppression of the enemy?"

As with a breaking of my bones, my enemies reproach me,
while they say to me all day long,
"Where is your God?"

Why are you cast down, O my soul?
And why are you disquieted within me?
Hope in God.
For I shall yet praise Him.
The help of my countenance and my God."
Psalm 42:9-11 NKJV

Thoughts From Aisle 7

It's cold in this aisle.

There is a caution sign on the floor
from thawed out ice cream and a tired heart.

My luck in picking men falls in the same category
as picking a shopping cart.

Loud and annoying.

Just stick my headphones in to drown it out.
Sing to me Jack Johnson, you beautiful creature.
You make love seem like a breeze.
Maybe one day I will get my *Banana Pancakes*.

Gladly will I shop for a frozen dinner for one.

Too tired to cook from picking up the mess you had made.

The checkout line is taking forever,
but I have nothing but time.

The good part of it all is I can toss this ridiculous buggy,
that is, until next time.

I Always Knew

Forever with him was never in my heart,
no matter how much I pretended.

I knew what he was, even when I didn't.

The Reasons I Left You

I made a list of all the times you could have said,
"No. I love my wife more than this."
When she called
When she walked inside our home
When you kissed
When you took your pants off
When you went to lie with her
When you gazed into her eyes and realized
they were not mine you were looking in to
Before you slipped into her.

100% Cotton

I wore the shirt today—
The shirt from two years ago that you got angry about
because it somehow shrunk.

I loved it.
It became mine.
The shirt I wore when I was sick.
The shirt I wore when I was sad.

It comforted me.

It kept me warm when I was cold.

It was comfortable.

It was all the things you never were.

As I put it on today, I thought, maybe I should throw it away
because of all the things you implanted in the shirt—

The things you couldn't be—
I don't want to wear it in public.

I don't want to give you a chance to see.

It's 100% cotton.

It's warm.

But I decided not to throw it away
because I haven't gotten around to replacing it yet.

Maybe because....

I don't want the shirt.
I want to burn it in a fire
and watch the ash float away to nothing.

And I don't want a shirt to replace what you didn't do—
I want the real thing.

A heart that's warm and wraps its arms around me—
That is—
If I wanted one at all.

The Ex Files

They are called exes.
The ones I choose to no longer have
in my own little circle that is my life.
But the parts that remain,
the parts that each one gave and each one took away.

Thank you to the one when I was 18.
The only one I knowingly did wrong to.
You gave me trust.
The only one, even now, that I might ever have that with.
The one who gave me love,
but I couldn't live with the stereotypical slogan of *D.A.R.E.*

Thank you to the one when I was 19,
who taught me about music, like the Black Crowes and Jimi.
You introduced me to my hippie side. I embrace it now.
The one who gave me the realization
that I choose men just like my father.
That is to say, sharing his worst trait of never saying "no."

Thank you to the plethora of ones in between
because believe me, there were plenty.
Don't get me wrong, I was never a Rahab.
And I always gave a two-week notice.

Thank you to the one at 23.
You lasted past the 14-day agenda.
Thank you for the fun.
Thank you for the friendship.
Thank you for your parents who helped save my soul.
Of you, I am thankful for the most.
Your parents helped me find my reason for life—that is Jesus.
You took my trust and gave me the present of heartache.

Thank you to the one from my late 20s.
You gave me the biggest trial of all.
That is to learn how to love the loveless.
You took my innocence.
You gave me Pandora's Box and made me open it.
Thank you for taking a piece of me that will never return.
Thank you for the fear of men you instilled in me.
Thank you for allowing me to never look at men
the same again.
Thank you for setting me free.

"In everything give thanks,
for this is God's will for you in Christ Jesus."
1 Thessalonians 5:18 NKJV

letters
..FROM..
THE
rosie
..CHRONICLES

To The Abuse Survivor

The worst thing they could have said was nothing.
The worst thing they could have done was nothing;
And they did exactly that, I know.
When what little left inside of you was screaming for mercy,
screaming for someone—anyone—to help,
but no one did because no one understood your message
that was delivered with smiles.

I know—
I know you don't want anyone to hurt—
You don't want anyone to feel pain—
I get it.

You are not crazy.
Yes, this happened to you.
I believe you. Listen to me, "I believe you."

You don't have to go further than your backyard
or your bedroom
to develop PTSD.
Soldiers are not the only ones who are given this curse.

There will be times you will want to do the
twelve steps of AA in reverse:

making a list of people who need to apologize
for just standing by;

but no amount of apologies will ever make what happened
to you okay.
No apology—not even his—will make living
with the aftermath of abuse bearable.

Some days you will be angry at him or
angry at yourself for allowing the abuse to happen,
but on those days, remember—
do all you can to remember—
that you are not the broken one.
You will survive this—I know because I did.

You are not damaged goods.
You are of value and lovely in the sight of God.

And always hang on to the truth that this body
that this heartless person has taught you to hate
will eventually turn to dust.

And your new spiritual body
will be one that no one will ever touch.

We Should Write A Song Together

I told this friend, we should write a song together.
"I'll come up with the lyrics, and you write the chords."

She asked me what was on my heart
to write a song about,

and I replied,
"That I never want to be made to feel like
I'm not enough again."

But We Can't Go Back

I want to go back to the innocence
of never having it in my mind that I could be abused...
just letting all things go and trust.
I want that so bad.

It was security. It was naïve.
Although I wish these things on no one,
it isn't fair that I have to always live with the fear
of it happening again.

Moving Forward

How do I overcome the abuse?
I am alone with this. No one understands it.
I pray not to be bitter about it
and not to harden my heart because of it.

Move forward.

That is what I try to tell myself.
Clean slate. A new and better beginning.

Do I just block the abuse out?

It was real.

No one will believe me.
They say, "What one person likes, the other doesn't."

Really?!

When your husband tells you, ********Explicit*********

That's not even the worst.
Not even a little.

How do I heal from abuse?
How do I get this out of my head?!
These unholy, wretched, sadistic flashbacks
that hollow me out to nothing again?

He called me at midnight the other night—
I didn't answer, but he kept on calling.

When I finally picked up the phone, he asked,
"Why do you want to talk to my sister?"

I wouldn't answer...
I don't want this on paper.

Evil—may evil never be repeated.
If only I could un-know what I know.

Dear Lord,
Help me to overcome—
Only You can.

Time Heals

I am afraid of men.
Afraid to be in a relationship
and even more terrified of marriage.

But a few things that I know to be true—
that this will pass and that I will love again
because my heart is too big not to.

The Aftermath

We are taught that Belle wins over the beast,
But why do we fail to warn her that a beast
can sometimes be only that?

Ripping through tissue, bone down to marrow,
leaving her with scars and not thinking twice about it.
If I wrote what I want to regurgitate out of my mouth;
what I want to scream—

I hate you.
I hate that you tainted my body—
That you used it like a toy.
No. Worse.
At least with toys,
you can clean them off and make them seem new again—
No. I am a car run through metal, chipped paint, ripped fabric,
broken windshield, dented beyond repair.

That is how I see my body now.
No shop can make it seem new again.
Progressive has declared the accident,
"Totaled beyond repair."
They say, "Here's a check—get a new one."
As if this were even an option.

This car is not worthy enough to have
as one left in the backyard of a trailer park.
It can't be fixed. It's used. It has lost its value.

The driver that I had trusted behind the wheel was reckless
and what's done is done.

Throw it out at Turkey Creek and never look back.

(Update: She is okay.)

Hush

Submission—
a beautiful thing to do when it comes to the Lord,
And the scariest thing to do when it comes to Ephesians 5.

If there was ever a word I despise,
that when said, my heart cringes and my nostrils flare.
A double meaning word that means beauty,
but also, shame, hurt, and fear.
But we don't talk about that.

The meaning of submission is not taught correctly,
not talked about, to be made silent
in a heart grown cold to the thought of it.
Something that men twist to their own likings,
to their own lust and fantasy.
But we don't talk about that.

I am not proud of the stripes I earned in submission.
My battle scars are too deep and too loud to cover
with a Band-Aid or a veil.
But we don't talk about that.

Appetizers

I am tired of people telling me that I am pretty.

Tired of giving pieces of my soul away to men
who never cared.
Of placing my whole self on a platter
as they treated me like a cheap meal.
Making me their main course,
then feeding their leftovers to the dogs.

Looks Aren't Everything

The truth is
most guys, spiritual or not, just want a girl that looks good.
But, I am too exhausted to care and compete with a world
I am not even meant to be in.

Row For One, Please

They say we walk together,
but it is hard for me to understand that
when I'm in a row of one made for twelve.

I fight this anger that when I walk alone,
I feel as though I am actually walking alone.

Every first day of the week
I become that girl in middle school
searching for somewhere to sit
in a cafeteria full of kids who don't get me
and who don't want to.

My heart longs for a row with someone.

So instead, I fight through the pain and I "pep talk" myself.
I tell myself that this row of one made for twelve
has no room for anyone else because
my heart fills every one of these chairs,
and to be patient, be kind, and to wait for the place
where no one stands alone.

Revealed

We were made for a purpose.
I was made with purpose—say this to yourself.
Repeat daily.

Write it on the bathroom mirror that you glance at
while brushing your teeth,
or when you look at yourself in it with shrugging shoulders
because you have not embraced your beauty yet.

Read these words and put them in your heart to be true
because they are...
Coming from someone who was once in shoes
similar to yours...

His voice telling you that you are worthless
will eventually get out of your head.

The distant memory of times past,
in the middle of doing nothing,
would rush in the shower only to use
hot water to try to burn and wash away
the skin he once touched.

The words that he penciled onto my body that said,
"Fat. Unintelligent. Typical. No good. Used.
Worthless. Unattractive."

They will slide off like water on a duck
never to be seen again,
on a body that is good,
that is beautiful.

letters about dragons

Splattered Ink

As I cry, I am aware that God knows
what is inside each tear drop:
each pain,
each loss,
each lie,
each ugly look received,
and He knows.

He keeps them and knows each one.
Vengeance is not mine, but I do know
that each tear that falls is splattered as ink on a page
that is yours for which you will give an account.

I hope that each tear drop pours out the hatred
that has seeped inside me because of you,
and I pray, eventually, I will have enough strength
to get rid of it all.

Due North

Sometimes I get tired of being nice to you.
I bite my tongue until it cuts and bleeds.

But, I know, that if I put aside my moral compass
and lose my way for only a moment,
I won't be happy because I will be just as lost

and cruel

as you.

Ebony

I am tired of weeping about ugly people.
If I could write you a letter, tell of all the things I keep inside,
I would say this:

I have seen your heart and it is as black as the night
with no stars to show a small glimmer of hope.

Your heart consists of pettiness and deceit.

Your words may hurt, but you cannot kill my soul.

Letters About Dragons

What can I say to You that has not already been spoken
in words out of my mouth, from my heart to You?

I turned away so that I might not see their face,
and now the dragon is breathing down the back of my neck
singeing hair, causing flesh to burn and crackle.

Be with me Lord, in my selfish ways, let me stay with You.
Calm my fears with Your presence.
Peel away my anger with Your tenderness.

Maybe I make things out to be so much more
than what they are sometimes.
I do not believe this is the case of "sometimes"—

Once the ink from my divorce papers dried,
I made a vow to myself that I would not let anyone
control me again.
I have now unwillingly lied to myself.

I mistakenly still faced the days with naïve ambitions
that I could help bring the good out in people.
I have now realized that my smile will not change the world—
not even this impossible soul.

Dear Father,

I cry out to You. Hear my plea.

One day, I will share this poem of prayer with the world.

Expose each Diotrephese that rolls across my path;

That twists the bones of the One who surrendered all.

I will, once again, write a letter entitled, "To the next victim"—

a letter I will, once again, never send.

Not My Battle

I tried to hold it in, but I felt the muscles in my eyes weaken
and my cheeks were touched by the salty rain —

Wipe it away.

Hide it like it never happened. As if you were unfazed.

Never let them see that they hurt you.
Never let them see that they got to you for even a moment,
clamped between their fist and palm.

Don't lose heart.

Remember that they are the ones that are empty.
They are the weak ones.
This isn't my battle.
This one, I will gladly put into the hands of my God.

Bitter Friendships

It later became a fragile mess
slow and painful walk on eggshells and splintered wood
I saw the ungrateful flaws of rust
and crooked nails between your smile and devious eyes.
It was like an "I'm ready" drop into the ash of the inevitable.

I hope the burn was worth the end.
But the part that stings, even still, is that I was used in your
fire that lit the night for you to run away.

letters
OF
Sweet
Nothings

Filters

Life in filters.
Cover it up with sepia tone deception.

Choose a filter—
Pick one or two—

Mix it together to cover up reality.

Give it some shade.
Make it look bright.
Keep it as a cover.

Whatever makes the momentary happiness seem credible,
as we stuff our insecurities and unmet expectations
in our pockets;

Button our hurt in a collared shirt,
mask our sorrow in shoe-laced sneakers,
and wrap it up with a lip stained grin.

So quick, pick a filter—
Make it vibrant and as blue as the ocean

that isn't blue at all.

To My Favorite Tree

There is something magical in how the leaves on a tree
will change their appearance to a crayon box full
of amber orange and burnt sienna right before they die,

Only to dance eloquently to the ground
to make room for something new.

Wake Up

I let my dreams take me away on a cloud that is not reality

my thoughts in REM, half asleep, half awake
have caused me to want to put on the glass slippers again,
only to once again find the shards of glass in my feet

and with the pain, I still won't wake up.

Discoveries

I have found that love is not always love,
happiness can be found in sadness,
God is my best friend,
that some people never say goodbye.

I have found forgiveness without repentance
is hard to let go.
That you can, in fact, feel the pain of a heart breaking,
That one is not the loneliest number.

I have found that most people live in between denial
and a confused smile.
I have found that we are all our own insecurities bottled up,
and that I don't need to go beyond myself to find love.

Paper Love Story

I am purchased as a gift for special occasions—
monogrammed, only to become a space-filler.
I am something that everyone has
just to say that they have me,
left out for display.

I have pages upon pages that have never seen the sunlight
or felt the fingertips of someone turning my pages.
I am the most popular book, yet the most unread.
This is where God's design meets a tragedy
of unwanting souls.

If only they would just listen and let my words fill their hearts,
and chip away the callused layers.

Let my love story unfold in your mind and discover,
that this love story I will tell you,
is ours.

Investments

Love is always a choice.
We choose who we talk to, who we invest in, who we like.

Loving someone is not like a magnet
that we are connected to, that draws us in.
We draw ourselves in.

If God gave us the option to love Him, then why would we
think that choosing to love people would be any different?

It isn't.
We are just people with excuses and bad reasoning.

Death

You do not hurt me—
You are the sting that will bring me home.

But for the ones who have not packed their bags,
For the ones who it will be more than a sting,
I hate you.

You are inevitable—
A realization I am not meant to stay here.

And I would rather blame you for taking the unprepared
but it really isn't your fault, is it?

Counting It All As Joy

You are my rain that makes me long to see a rainbow.

You are the one teaching me a lesson
that I never cared to have.

Nevertheless, I am at peace with your presence,
but only after the swelling has gone down
and the color purple has turned into a jaundiced yellow.

I don't always like to open my door to you.
I never sent you an invitation.

But once you have left,
I am thankful that you came.

You are the thunderous rumbling
of the clouds over a stormy ocean.
Tossing and turning me in my boat,
with the light tower always in view
to give me that ray of something better.

There are reasons you invited yourself
that even I can't figure out.

But I always trust that you will get me
to the other side of hope.

"My brethren, count it all joy when you fall into various trials,
Knowing that the testing of your faith produces patience."
James 1:2-3 NKJV

Dear Local Bookstore

I found your section of poetry
totaling only about forty books tonight

But, they gave the right amount of room for me to sit in awe.

Each book, page, word, and letter written is to be felt
with eyes, with ears, with soul.

When I make enough money,
I will buy each one of those books at least once,
so that you may continue to think it is a good idea
to keep this section alive.

Could you? For me?

So that I may walk to this spot, sit once more,
shut out all the people surrounding me,
all the elevator music on the overhead,
and listen as the words from the poets' hearts enter mine.

letters to: L.A.

Things I Know To Be True

I don't trust that someone can love me,
But I trust that God does.

I don't trust in tomorrow,
But I trust that God will meet me there.

I don't trust. I never really have.

Since 24, when I first called Him My Father,
I always longed to go home.
I never knew happiness for long—only heartache—
and I had enough of that to last a lifetime.

I was done at the age of 24.
And now, at the age of 33,
I don't trust that anyone can love me,
But I trust that God always will,
and that's all I ever really wanted.

Wondering

I have my mother's hands so when I look at them, I smile.
I have an infectious laugh.
I am an unsinkable ship.

I have too many feelings,
so much that my feelings have feelings.

I randomly laugh out loud.
I laugh at my own jokes as I am telling them
before I can even get the punch line out.

I have compassion.
I could hug for days.

...and Jesus commands us to love as **you love yourself**.
Loving myself isn't my issue.

My problem is wondering why others don't.

Daisies

This girl has a free spirit, with flowers in her hair
Free to laugh, free to roam, free to love if she dares.

Because Enough Of My Past Life Was Spent In Doing As The Gentiles

Better to be alone with God in my room on a Saturday night, than at a place surrounded by people where God is not.

Don't Send Me Flowers

Every beginning's end starts with flowers.

My dad gave me a dozen roses when I was twelve and they
were the last gift I remember getting from him.
The smell of an orchid is the smell of death.

My grandmother's funeral—flowers
My dad's cremation day—flowers

My first boyfriend surprised me by placing flowers
on my car at school—that is when I knew we were over.

A guy friend sent me flowers at work—
I was so embarrassed.
I tried selling the flowers, then quickly ended the friendship.

In lieu of flowers at my funeral,
I request a *bouquet of newly sharpened pencils*
and when it's over, gift them to my favorite schools
with a note that reads, "Never stop writing."

All this to say, I do not like flowers.
I'm not a typical girl that wants to be lavished with objects
that smell like formaldehyde.

Although, I am like a flower in the way that I bloom
when the time is right,
and I need to be showered with love and sunlight to survive.

But I am not dead nor do I smell like it,
and if you send me flowers, I will shed a petal to say
"Goodbye."

When Emotions Are
Your Super Power

This sucks sometimes.
I take on other people's pain like it's my own.
I don't want them to be alone with it.
I wear it like my favorite sweater that makes me want to eat
ice cream and crawl back into bed.

Tell me it's okay.

Tell me it's okay to feel this much.

Maybe if I tried not to care, things would be easier.
Hebrews 3 repeats in the same chapter,
"Not to harden our hearts."
I listen to these words and exhale
as the tears fall slowly down my cheeks.

But because I feel pain, I also feel immense joy.

That is when I see a rainbow in the middle of a dark, gray sky.

A colorful rainbow full of hope.

Persistence

I fail daily
But I am thankful that I serve the One who is bigger
than my fears.

He gives me mercy when I deserve death.
He gives me love when I practice hate.
His patience and grace cover me like a blanket,
Atoning for all my sins that I beg to be forgotten.

Each morning I wake,
I thank God for giving me another day to make it all right—
To try again
To live a life worthy to be called His child.

I will never be worthy,
But I will never stop trying.

To God Be The Glory

So I write.
I mix words together to capture the combination
of heart, mind, and imagination.

But if I don't give the glory to the One who gave me this gift,
then I have only mixed together empty words full of vanity.

Expectations

I sometimes feel as though I am transparent—
through my fair skin I reveal my hurt,

Through this freckle on my hand,
I reveal that I am an abuse survivor,

My long locks of brown hair,
reveal the young girl inside me, longing to be held,

Behind my smile,
I reveal my insecurities,

And behind it all,
I reveal unmet expectations.

Pillows And Promises

I have to stop pushing people away;
how easily I can fall into this bed of loneliness
and oversized pillows.

But I will make a promise to myself that I have to leave
the pillows neatly organized as I walk away,
and allow people to love me.

True Story

When a woman shows her left hand,
ring out for the world to see,

Others see beauty and new adventures,
I see a glistening cage in 14-karats.

No One Is An Island

They tell me that no one is an island,
but how is it that I can feel the sand between my toes?
Feel the rushing of the ocean waves wash onto my feet?
I guess it was only the puddles of tears I have shed in silence.

No one is an island, that is what they tell me;
Yet, all I ever see are smiling faces as the word "good"
is passed out like candy.
My heart, I place in my hands for someone to touch,
to want, to love, but I am what they say no one is.

Anxiety

is a sickness I cannot get rid of.
The heart beats fast and my breathing becomes heavy.
If feelings were seasons, anxiety would be all year round,
Creeping through my bones as the blood rains.

My Cup Overflows

The Word tells us that we should bear one another's burdens,
thus, fulfilling the law of Christ.

I have burdens of pain that I call my own.
It is my pain, but it is not my pain to keep.

It is my pain to share.
Pride needs to fall off me—

shed like scaly skin to reveal my layer of pain
that I will try not to bear alone.
Without pain, I would not understand joy completely.

I would not appreciate the art of joy
without knowing heartache as I have.

Not to share my pain is to not share joy
that comes at the moment I think that

the pain will last a lifetime.
I am not sugarcoated.

I am like a stem of grapes: sweet yet bitter.
Let me fill your cup with my pain.

Let me fill your cup with my joy.

All in one, in order for me to fulfill my duties as a servant.

As a soldier.

As a child of God.

The Love Letter: Part I

Dear Lisa,

I saw you look into the mirror today and for the first time in a long time, you looked at yourself and thought, in your heart, "I'm really not that overweight." Good for you.

You are finally tearing away the shame and guilt and heartache that has for so long been in you when you look in the mirror. Again I say, good for you.

You are not crazy. You are a hopeless romantic. You see the good in others and can't even imagine that there is bad. You are a woman. You are a loving woman.

A radiant, good-spirited woman who does not tear others down. You treat others with mercy and kindness.

Even in your worst, you find ways to smile. This is one of your most admirable traits.

You have been broken. You have been abandoned all your life, and have never been enough for anyone.
Stop saying that!

You are enough for yourself. You are enough for God.
You love when you get no love in return. What a wonderful servant of God you are. It's okay to be alone. You won't hurt yourself as others have hurt you.

Decorate your house exactly as you envision it to be. Love how you want. You can say "no" and not care.
You submit only to the Lord—who is all majesty and will never leave you or lead you astray.

When you look in the mirror, the Almighty God will not cloud your sight with shame, impurity, or disgust, but rather, He will embrace you with love, grace, strength, peace, and hope.

You will smile genuinely and love all you want. You are beautiful on the outside, and much, much more on the inside because as Proverbs says, *"A woman who fears the Lord is to be praised."*

Because you serve the one true God, you have a beauty that never fades.

When you walk in a room, your glow shines like no other.
Jesus loves you.

He died for you because you are worth dying for. He has a place for you in Heaven, and no one can take that from you.

I love you.

Love,
Lisa Ann

"However difficult it may be, think of positive things.
Think of the good things of you.
Dig deep, and write yourself a letter."
Loida

Until Now

September 16, 2006, I became a child of the true living God.
Buried with Christ in baptism, He washed away the guilty sod.

I knew what Christ did for me, and I knew all the facts.
The whole Bible is about love, and one, true,
forever-selfless act.

See, I knew Christ died for me in order
to be able to go to that heavenly land,
I understood He was the perfect sacrifice,
but that's not the problem at hand.

It has taken me eight years of my life with Christ
to fully understand my worth.
To truly grasp how He left His throne in Heaven
to come to this earth.

This isn't some small task; He did have the ability to sin.
He took a chance on losing Heaven for me,
He could have let Satan win.

Starting in Genesis it tells how it all began.
God created us, knew we would sin,
and had an amazing plan.

What Christ went through on this earth, all the agony,
It really shows and proves His love,
especially for sinners like me.

At a young age by the examples set before me,
I learned I wasn't deserving of love,
at least from what I could see.

But as I grow in Christ, He sweetly tells me
that I am worth it all,
As He holds my hands through the fire,
in hopes that I don't fall.

No man, no person on this earth will ever again
make me feel like I do not matter.
It wouldn't make sense because Christ is my life,
their talk is worthless chatter.

No matter what life throws at me,
I know God will forever be there.
He tells me, *"Never will I leave you, nor forsake you,"*
just come to Me in prayer.

"But now, thus says the Lord, who created you,
O Jacob, and He who formed you,
O Israel: Fear not, for I have redeemed you;
I have called you by your name; you are Mine.
When you pass through the waters, I will be with you;
And through the rivers, they shall not overflow you.
When you walk through the fire,
You shall not be burned.
Nor shall the flame scorch you.
For I am the Lord your God."
Isaiah 43:1-3 NKJV

A Friendly Reminder

I think we are forever healing,
just don't dwell on the past.

You got away from the unfaithful.
You have a chance at life beyond what he could never give
and what he took away.

Dwell on the blessings that God gives
that overflow in abundance.
That are like the sands of the sea.

An eternity with the One who loved you first (and always).

You were made for somewhere other than this.
You knew this before you really did.

Dwell on God.
Dwell on good.

He is always there to lead you,
You just have to let Him.

"Finally, brethren, whatever things are true,
whatever things are noble, whatever things are just,
whatever things are pure, whatever things are lovely,
whatever things are of good report,
if there is any virtue and if there is anything praiseworthy—
meditate on these things."
Philippians 4:8 NKJV

The Love Letter: Part II

Sweet Lisa,

Hello beautiful. I say "beautiful" because you are.

You found yourself again—or really for the first time.

You are living, loving, and are not in a box.

Please remember. Always remember—
no one can put you in a box without your consent—
and you will never consent to it.

Zephaniah 3 : 17 says,
"He will quiet you with His love.
He will rejoice over you with singing."

God will! He does! The Almighty Creator!
He quiets you with His love, Lisa.

So, to let a man on this earth put you in a box
and control you again is revolting!

God, the Creator doesn't, so why would you
let anyone do that? You wouldn't.

The Creator of Heaven and Earth rejoices over you with song!

Know. Your. Worth.

Know, if a man—not a boy—a man, comes to you—
or if God blesses you with one,
or deems it necessary to have a friend—do not settle.

List what you want and if he is not that—then walk away.

The list is as follows...

letters

TO

Side kicks

Paul

You were my first of a lot of things.
I still think of you when I see sugar cubes, when I think of
theology class or never making it to school dances.
Endless phone conversations never ending with goodbye,
but with either your mom or mine picking up the phone
and saying,
"It's a school night. Go to bed."
Kids with no clue about life.
A girl who wasn't yet defined.
A boy trying to find himself.
A girl who liked you, but was too easily annoyed with
immaturity being your strong suit, but why did I expect
anything different?
We were punk kids acting like punk kids.
We were dreamers.
Summers in a room filled with baseball cards and
awkwardness.
Looking back on those years, I realize,
you were my high school.
I'm sorry I quit you.

Andy

I want to remember tonight for always;
Purchase its memories in the gift shop of my mind.
Bottle it up in a snow globe,
Shake it up and watch the words float down in the essence of
its raw beauty.
My receipt from the night is printed with the exchange of real
emotion from a tired but optimistic man—
A hopeless romantic with his arms stretched out to catch love
like butterflies.

The Return

The innocence returned.
It never really left.
Snatched away in the night by a blue-eyed monster.

It returned to me.
Engulfed my heart.

I broke that brick wall, grabbed that little girl by the hand, and
laced her up for battle.

Now she is clothed with the armor of God.

And that girl—who grew to be complete in Christ—smiles.
And her heart is complete in Him.
It is wrapped in the most perfect blanket,
covered in righteousness.

All the ugliness that tried to overtake the things she would later
do that seemed 'normal'—have been washed away;
So that the purity of her heart is tucked in
with the most wonderful of all love.

She doesn't need someone to call home.
HE is her heart—she just had to open the door.

"The Lord also will be a refuge for the oppressed.
A refuge in times of trouble.
And those who know Your name will put their trust in You;
For You, Lord, have not forsaken those who seek You."
Psalm 9:9-10 NKJV

To My Baby Sister's Babies

A few things I want you to know.

1.
Time is precious and should be spent wisely.
It is one of the most cherished and memorable gifts you can give someone.

See, time never stops, it breathes in and out, and we count time by stargazing at night, and tracing our fingers around the shapes of clouds in the day.

2.
People will come and go like seasons. Spring for allowing relationships to bloom. Summer for when you want to bask in the glow of their beauty. Fall for the ones you want to sit on a park bench with and say nothing. Winter for the harsh, bitter lessons in love.

All seasons have their peaks and valleys. I know your heart is tender like mine, which probably means you will want to keep a season forever, even when they must leave. Let the tears fall and say goodbye. It's going to be okay because each season teaches us something new. Just be careful not to look past the people who are not seasons, but are here to stay.

3.

People will disappoint you. People are not perfect.

So for the times they cause the sides of your mouth
to point south, always be ready to forgive.

Sometimes the battle is not about you, but you will get tossed
in the fight. For this, I am sorry.

4.

I pray for you and think of you more times than I think I blink in
a day.

5.

Always choose good, even when it's not easy.

6.

God loves you. God is never changing. His love is what will
bring you through life. I pray you find God faster than I did.
And I will be here if you want me to help.

Your Season

And if I were only with you for a season,
let me be your Fall.

Watch me as I change colors before your eyes,
Leaves falling in the same way I did for you.
Sit beside me for a little while, if it's only a little while,
red leather jacket and mismatched socks.

Wear me like your favorite sweater,
so that when the wind blows,
you need only me to keep you warm.

Boy, sweet boy, thank you for the chance to experience
something I have not felt in a decade.
Thank you for letting me be your season.

When winter comes, you will still remember me,
as if I would always come back to you,
even if only for a little while.

Mikey

You don't have to wait to be someone magnificent;
You already are.

You just need to choose to let love in.
Not all at once.
Let it shine through the spaces between each shutter on the
blinds of your windows.
Let it slowly warm the room.
One day, when you pull the string to let it all in,
Then you will be ready.

And your heart will smile when you finally embrace the love
that has always been there,
waiting for you to say,
"Hello."

Because it is hard to transition, here come the rhymes...

Loida: My Forever Friend

We weren't strangers when we met,
we had a connection from the start.
I believe God put us together;
you will forever have a place in my heart.

2,045 miles from my home to yours seems so far away,
but just know we can always look up at the same sky,
night or day.

Like Piglet and Pooh, Barbie and Ken,
We make a really good team,
you make a really great friend.

So when we are vintage and gray, rocking in our chairs,
I know no matter where I am, you will be there.

To My Favorite Katie

Someone who makes you smile,
who laughs at all the jokes you say,
Someone you can learn with, study with,
and pray

Someone whose love runs deep
Someone who will listen to the secrets that you keep

Someone you can lean upon when your life is full of sadness
Who isn't big on hugs, but will give them with gladness

Someone who shares your interest at heart
Someone who stays in touch, even though you live far apart

Someone who you can be yourself with all the time
Someone who tells you she loves hearing your rhymes

In short, everyone needs a friend that is wonderful and true
Everyone needs a "Katie"
I'm glad mine
is you.

Trace

You say people look at you like you are crazy,
But I think that their sight is kind of hazy.

See, God looks at the heart of man
while man looks at the outer appearance
what seems to be normal
is simply a false deliverance.

You are going to be okay,
I know you will as long as you put God on your side,
So, sit back, relax, and enjoy the ride.

My sweet little Trace,
some others might think differently of you,
but I know that you are a treasure and more importantly,
God does too.

Don't let others' dictate the way you live your day to day
Just be true to God in all that you do and say.

And if I can just tell you one more thing
before I end this rhyme,
I love that God decided to make you my nephew,
I'm here for you anytime.

Davis: Welcome To The Book Club

Oh, the places you will go with those big, brown eyes
Never knowing where the next page's destination lies

With each book that opens your mind to a new place,
Remember to read the book at your own pace,
for it is not a race

When you meet people holding a book you once read,
they won't be strangers anymore
For you will have shared adventures
because your eyes have opened the same door

I hope you will pass on your love for books
to Belle and Ruby Judy Lou,
Just like your Dad did for Sam, and now you will, too!

#thebookclubkids

Curly Top

Don't ever dull your sparkle and always live out loud little one
When others try to knock you down,
twirl that dress and soak up the sun

Sing with all you've got, let it come from the heart
The world is a great adventure, life is art

God made you so precious, so unique
From your curly top, down to your little feet

Most of all remember to whom you belong,
Look for the good in others, life is one big song

*When Belle, at age five, took my hand on Sunday morning and whispered,
"Do you want to see me twirl?"*

Rhett

When I see your face,
I think, "It's good to see my friend."

When you help me with the problems of life,
I know I have a friend 'til the end.

Because you deserve your own rhyme.

Realization

Love is NOT forced.
Love comes from the One, true source.

No one on this earth will ever be able
to fill that place in my heart
Only God, the Creator can;
the One who loved me from the start.

Of course, it is Him, how could I be so blind?
The One who would never leave me, abuse me,
or treat me unkind.

It is not your fault, little girl sitting on the brick wall,
that you were not shown love;
But I am showing you what it is now.
Listen to me, it's from God above.

Never settle for someone just because they come along.
Realize your worth, keep the faith, stay strong.

If God never gives you a man
to treat you like a true Christian man should,
Then stay content with yourself.
If God wanted you to have a man, then you would.

"My flesh and my heart fail; But God is the strength of my heart and my portion forever."
Psalm 73:26 NKJV

letters to Strangers

Til' The Beginning

They tell you that there is cancer in your bones, but what they
don't see is God's grace and love spreading throughout your
soul calling you gently home.

So lay your anxiety to rest and fall asleep in His arms.
We all long to be where there is no night, so do not fear;
We will all be together again, in the beginning.

The Social Butterfly

Only what the eyes can see:
white teeth, bleached hair,
fair skin, with the best clothes to wear.

Name brands (no generics), full tank of gas,
dermatologist approved,
give it a year,
you will get fake boobs.

Fifty likes within one minute,
that's what makes your heart leap,
No substance, a brilliant facade of things that will not keep.

Use people at your leisure,
keep them as tools in organized, dirty jars
next to your $50 products for your bleached hair,
whitening teeth kit, but that's only what the eyes can see.

The surface is only skin deep,
in the end that is not what is going to sustain.
What's inside of the girl that only thinks of the appearance,
only cares about what will not remain?

Wonderfully Made

Sing O' barren one,
Your womb may be closed, but your heart is far from it.
The doctors tell you that you do not have all the necessary
parts—but your veins have life and love flowing in them.

And although it is not for two,
God knows what you can bear and what you cannot.
He formed you.
He knows you.
He made you exactly how you were meant to be.
He does not make mistakes
And though you have none to call your own,
you are loved by them all.

Cleansing The Soul

It's okay to let the teardrops fall.
Let them fall in the hands that are home.

He collects every tear.
No sufferance is in vain.

Close your eyes.

Let the salty liquid of pain flow down and
fall beautifully in His palms.

Let it cleanse the soul.
Let delight now run through your veins.

Let the tears fall.

Once it is all dried and done, see God shine through the
twinkling of purified eyes that are brighter than any star.

"You number my wanderings; Put my tears into Your bottle;
Are they not in Your book? When I cry out to You,
Then my enemies will turn back; This I Know, because God is for me."
Psalm 56:8-9 NKJV

letters {to} co-dependents

What Remains

It astounds me how some people can toss others around
seamlessly like the waves of the blue.
How they are apathetic as they walk away, while the victim is
left with the shattered remains.

Normal

Because to her, this is normal
Memories of a childhood finding syringes around the house,
and we call it "normal"
And if Dad were alive,
and he asked me one thousand times to forgive him,

I would

I think a daughter is always desperate
for the love of her father.
Mom taught us to give up ourselves for a man
because that's what she did, and she called it "love"

But You Knew That Already

Dear Girl,
You knew you couldn't of stayed with him, right?
They say, once a person gets sober,
they can never stay sober with the person they were with
before. You knew this, right?

He could have never stayed sober with you.
This is not to say you were the problem.
This is to say he had to blame someone.
When he would gaze into your eyes,
he was looking at the whites of your eyes
and craving the next hit.

If he read this, he would probably
start thinking of having to return his AA coin.
The addict can never stay with anyone.

He didn't love you. He couldn't.
How could he when he was in love with substance?

You knew he didn't love you, right?
This is not to say you are not loveable.
This is to say; you chose to love a boy who didn't know how
to love anyone except himself.

And They All Fall Down

Do you ever feel as though **addiction** is an unforgiveable sin?
Causing thievery of heart, body and soul; not only to the one
who chose it, but the ones who were around in the wake.
Watch them all fall with the addict's back towards them,
and the ones who can't help but love, be trampled under foot.

You Can't Blame The Boy

As young girls, we think that the love we have for the guy
who says those three words are different;
That our love is the love that will shake the world,
Prove we are what God was talking about in Genesis 2.
We are naïve to think that we won't be deceived in the next
chapter–
Pick that fruit off of a tree that is not ours to pick and wrap it
up with an apology.

"But baby, our love is the type of love
that will shake the world."
How can we be so naïve to think
this is what we were made for?
This love that would never lie, or cheat, or steal the innocence
of a girl who believed so hard that she could be enough.

Boys are selfish.
Boys steal things and never say they are sorry for it.

The twinkle in that girl's eyes will fade into shooting stars,
burned out with the realization she will never be enough for
him to stay sober.

Love Doesn't Fix Selfishness

I have this journal—
I keep it locked up, but I never throw it away.
I hold it in my hands tonight, knowing each page inside
was written by a tired soul of a woman desperately hanging
onto a promise.

Some men seem destined for greatness, for showing love,
service, and for being what God wants them to be—
but this book is not about those types of men.

Those men do not exist in her story.
No, this one is about a man destined to become the monster;
climbing walls and breathing fire on hearts.

If I handed you this book and said, "This will be you in a few
years if you don't run" would you believe me?

If I tell you that love doesn't fix selfishness, or no man should
ever curse at you, or make you feel like you are less than you
are, would you believe me?

If you opened your eyes to see that is how he treats you,
would you run then?

The Ripple Effect

It all starts with one.
And once it takes place, it can't be undone.

It's a depressing thought knowing how it can affect people
Through sin and hypocrisy with some hiding in the building with
a steeple.

We are all human and we all fall short of the glory of Him;
All because we decided to trade our crown for an hour of sin.

When we allow the heart to become hard
is when the waves start coming in
Those waves can take others too before their life even begins.

But the waves can stop when we set in our hearts
for the cycle to break
We have to face reality,
no matter how much it makes the heart ache.

Time stops for no man, of this I'm sure.
Break the cycle, live for God, He will help us to endure.

We can overcome the hardships that this life gives us whether
we are big or small

Remember, no one ever said it would be easy, but Heaven is most certainly worth it all.

"There is no fear of God before his eyes.
For he flatters himself in his own eyes,
when he finds out his iniquity and when he hates.
The words of his mouth are wickedness and deceit.
He has ceased to be wise and to do good.
He devises wickedness on his bed,
he sets himself in a way that is not good;
he does not abhor evil."
Psalm 36:1-4 NKJV

letters TO God

A Seal Of Our Union

Dear Lord,
The day I stop living for you is the day I become empty.
Instead, let me empty my soul out to You;
Live in between the safety of Your love
and the uncertainty of the day.

A.C.T.S.

Dear Lord,
When teaching the children how to pray, I went down a list of
helpful hints and said:

Adoration – strong feelings of love.

Confession – to know that my sins are ever before me
and I must confess and turn from them.

Thanksgiving – always thankful for what I have
and what I do not.

Supplication – to ask earnestly and humbly.

Dear Lord, I must stop and say that I am thankful that I am no
longer fearful of waking up in the mornings next to the person
who once laid beside me.

A Place To Call Home

Without Him I am empty;
A pulse with a cold heart.
A child scared of the dark.
A lost soul with no hope.

Dear God,
You rescued me from the pit of despair.
From the tight grip of Satan – You shined Your light upon me
and my heart could not resist the warmth of Your love, and it
added to my pulse, a hopeful heart, and a place to call home.

Undeserving

Dear Lord,
I am struggling to find the right words to say –
in these times I am thankful that You can hear my heart and
understand what I struggle to put into words.
Dear God,
I love You –
I love that with You, my heart can stay calm in knowing that I
am enough for You, even though I am undeserving.

Ephesians 5:2

Please, Lord – let me do this right.

*"And walk in love, as Christ also has loved us
and given Himself for us, an offering and a
sacrifice to God for a sweet-smelling aroma."
Ephesians 5:2 NKJV*

Until You Do

I rest in the peace that You promised,
and I wait, most of the time impatiently,
for You to take my hand,
and bring me home.

Until You do,
I will praise You where I stand,
Cry out to You where I lay,
And hold onto Your promises everywhere I go.

When It's Not Okay

I apologize for what I am about to say.
Sometimes. Right now.
I am a bitter cup of ugly.

These wicked thoughts cause my heart to turn shades of
ebony, speckled with hatred, envy, bitterness.
All things in which I try not to have when they cover my eyes,
blind to the truth.

Dear God, my soul is Yours.
My heart is Yours.
And when it is time for me to return these used goods of me,
I pray,
I will give them back and be forever in Your light.

Home

Even in the darkest of times,
Lead me towards Your light and bring me Home.

Lord's Supper Thoughts

Right now, at this moment, **nothing else matters**—
In a room full of people, You and I are the only ones here.

You are my love and my life
Help me to trust—
Remind my heart that You go before me, stand beside me,
will protect me from harm.
Jesus knew **every detail** of His death and pain,
and He still died for me.

To know that while I was being abused,
You were holding my hand,
assuring me that **I would survive this**.

What happened to me will make me stronger in You,
so that when the race is finished,
my prize will be me in Your arms.

The Lord's Supper

I am not worthy of this
And my first instinct is to run and hide—just like Eve.
But I cannot hide from You, and in my heart,
I know that I would rather run to You.

Keep me safe in Your love, and help me to never stray
But "never" is almost impossible for the flesh, so instead,
when I fall, when I make some of my biggest,
shameful mistakes,

Help me to face my wrongs and instead of heeding to them,
I shall run into Your arms of grace.

During The First Day Of The Week

Dear Father,
Allow me to free my mind of all my surroundings,
to lean upon You.

Comfort me.
Let me lay upon Your chest and fall asleep in Your arms.

You keep me safe.
I cannot live without You.
Without You, I am only flesh and bones.
With You, I am a soul, a precious soul.
Help me to clear my mind of all the discouragements,
all the lives that know You not.

Dear Lord,
Calm my worried heart.
Thank You for Jesus, for risking Heaven for me;
for doing what no one else could do.

I need You every moment.
A moment without You is only empty space
and meaningless time.

L.A.

Joy

Today I am joy.
I will choose to live in it.
Keep joy stamped on my heart and call out Your name

with thanksgiving.

Always Your daughter,

Lisa Ann

Isaiah 53

You are my favorite in all the world, in all the Heavens,
and our love story is my favorite.

You are my constant in a world of change.
When all things feel lost,
I look up and peace comes over me knowing that You have a
place for me, reserved for me, and in a world of thievery,
no one can take my home with You away.
You make my soul to sing and calm my worried heart.
Forever with You is my heart's desire.
You are beside me when I think I am alone.
I want to be all I can be for You—please help me to be.
Let my spirit return to You, my flesh turn to ash,
my soul forever beside You.

Promises

Your promises will lead me Home.
In the dark, You are my light, and always, You are my way.
There is nothing that You cannot do.
Help me to trust only in You.
I want to land on the clouds as I fall into Your love.

Overcome

Dear Lord,
I am undeserving of Your love.
As I take part in remembering Your sacrifice, who am I?
A selfish person.
Someone who limits You.

Dear Father in Heaven,
You tell me that "all things are possible" with You
I must believe that all these trials have a purpose
and that You will see me through them.

At times, I feel as though I am alone with my battles.
I am scared of men.
Help me to overcome these things.
I love You.

My Kind Of Love

That is the kind I hold on to with all of my being.

That is the love that I fully trust, that gives me peace at night.

The love that shines through my windows in the morning
and warms my soul.

The love that awakens me in the nap time of the day.

The love that makes my soul sing.

That makes my soul come alive.

The love that made my soul.

"I have loved you with an everlasting love."
Jeremiah 31:3 NKJV

New Words

Your love, from somewhere that seems so far, is next to me.

Embedded in my heart.

Your fingertips swirl in the sky to form the clouds for mirth.

Clouds and moon that allow me to see
the work of Your hands.
This isn't even the beginning of the beauty of the creations
You have made.

And who am I but thankful,
that You have put a new song in my heart?

The words I write are no longer of men's folly,
but of the splendor of You and Your mercy on me.

My love and my God.
I am in awe of You.

Longing

But the hairs on my head are counted, and my tears, like rain,
God so lovingly bottles up in a jar.
Not one drop is in vain.

His grace and mercy intertwine with the beauty of His love
that I am undeserving of.

Actions speak when words are silent.

The Son of God, risking eternal life with the Father,
for someone so undeserving.
Each time that I sin, I drive those nails in deeper.
I cannot live without my Lord.

Some say it's a choice.
Not living for Him is not an option for me.
Once I tasted what the Lord had to offer, I knew I would never
be the same.
And I will always long to go home.

Lisa's Song

I want my first breath in the morning to shout Your name.

Whispers won't do.
And as Your name pumps from my heart,
throughout my soul, let it physically be said from my mouth.

Let it roll off my tongue with joy and adoration.
Thankfulness and exaltation.

And although I would rather be in Heaven,
I will gladly beg of You to use me as Your instrument,
Your voice on this Earth.

The Words of Truth, as they leap off the pages, come alive
with each word spoken — may I have the ability to teach
others the only way to truly live.

My body may grow tired, but oh, my soul.
My soul will never stop until I am resting peacefully
in Abraham's bosom.

Then, when the trumpet sounds, I will forever sing Your
praises and never grow weary.

These are my thoughts when I rise in the morning;
For at night, when I lay my head down, I tell You of my day.

I thank You. I praise You.

And as I fall asleep praying to You, my Father in Heaven,
I feel as though I am drifting to sleep
in the comfort of Your hands.

And as I sleep, I sleep peacefully in Your safety.

And when I awake,
I shout Your name,
Because whispers will never do.

Even Still

You brought me through the tears.
The nights I had to learn how to sleep alone again,
You were there.

When it was time for the moon to glow, and the stars to
shine, and I still slept on the right side of my queen-sized bed
that was now for one, You held me through the night.
I never got cold because You were my comforter.

The days when I got hurt, You bandaged my wounds, for
Your Words were what healed me.

Years later,
when it seemed as though everyone was miles away,
When I silently screamed, "No,"
You said, "It's okay. Stay with Me. I won't let go."

And today,
when it seems as though everything
is about to be taken away,

When I'm shoved in a corner—I lift my hands to You in praise,
and You safely take me away.

letters

TO Maybe

ONE DAY

Percentages

I can't give you my whole heart; it belongs to the One who has reserved a place for me in Heaven.

What I can give you is a part of my heart that will be loyal, kind, and understanding.

I'm not going to give you a fairytale.
But, I will try to be everything that God has asked me to be for you.

As Dreamers Do

I want a forever that can write poetry so beautifully that I
cannot express just how beautiful they are.
I want a forever who looks at me the way a woman longs to
be gazed upon: sweetly and honest.
I want a forever who makes loving him easy.
I want a forever that I won't have to question his love.
I want a forever who holds me when I'm scared and is okay
with me stealing the covers at night.
I want a forever with a kind heart and a country accent.
I want a forever who calls me lovely
and teaches me to like compliments.
I want a forever, but I'm okay with dreaming for now.

To Neverland

It's not that I ever wanted to grow up
Circumstances forced me into it.
But no matter the age, I still want adventure.
I still want laughs and endless smiles.
Life is too short on earth
and it's too exhausting to waste any time not living.

Passports

I don't want to see the world
or ever own a passport for that matter.

I have seen all that I have desired to
and I am satisfied with watching the grass grow
in my own back yard, slow like evergreen,
weeds sprouting, dandelions whispering wishes in the wind.

I have seen all but one thing.

I know what you want to tell me,
that there is so much more than Alabama.
And that, sure, it's sweet,
but there is riper fruit in warmer places.
I don't doubt this, but a pillow of contentment
layered with a blanket of "I am enough"
is what I lay myself upon every night.
Now don't misunderstand me when I tell you
that I would like to be your company.
You see, you are the "one thing" I have left to see.

I just want to see myself in your eyes
and know that I am safe,
and that my eyes are the only destination you will ever crave.

One Day

One day I will be enough.
And my heart will be enough for the one
who is meant to love me.

Ya See, It's Like This

Just stop.
I need to stop fighting for a love that I really don't want.
I don't want that! I know I don't want that.
Why go back to something that is used and worn
simply because it is familiar?
Being familiar does not make it good.

You see, I am fine by myself.
I am okay with being alone.
But God did not make us to be like hermit crabs
who crawl back in their shell at the hint of a sunbeam.
But instead, to have the windows down,
sunrays hitting the glow of my cheeks
that causes sadness to sweat out of my body
to never return.

He made us to be "a people." A people who are not alone.
A church is people. A church cannot be just one.
And if a woman is considered to be a crown to a man,
than I shall sparkle and gleam with the best of them.

What I am saying is that I want love to give me a chance
for a change.

Have the arrow pointing at *my* heart with *his* hope being
that he could win my love,
the way that I could fall into his without even trying.

But just know, this road with me will not be easy,
and that I will always be waiting on the day
that you walk out and never come back.
Or the day you tell me you accidently fell into someone else
like the rest did, with your pants around your ankles,
over and over again.

And I will ask questions that I will never have a 100% answer
for, like, "What do you want for dinner?"
or "What should I wear?"
But, to the other questions that do matter,
I will learn to love something new about you everyday.

All this to say, I want you, but maybe I don't.
And I will always be indecisive,
but that's a part of me that makes me a woman, right?

And my heart will be scared, but know this,
If my heart gave you a chance, then you must be worth it.

The Existence Of Love
Or Lack Thereof

My problem is not that I do not think that love exists.
I know that it does.

Every time that I see a parent hold their child, or the way a
woman's husband will reach to hold her hand first, spread out
his fingers and make them fall in love with hers as they rest in
each other's palms.

I know that love is not merely a feeling. Feelings fade.
No, love is a verb. A sacrifice. An "I want to have you in my
arms, so just fall into them, but even if you don't, even if you
reject me, I will love you all the more."

I know that love is all around.
The problem is that love does not exist for me.
So I will choose to, I will plead to, learn how to live in the
middle of contentment and heartache;
that even though love does not exist for me,
it does in fact exist.

Translating When I Say "You Are Not My Type"

I am not ready
But if you are willing to wait,
I will meet you there.

Verbs

I am not yours to have unless God brings us in union.
Being a Christian does not give me the vaccination to withhold
the desires that my body wants.

I am human.
I am not as strong as I seem,
but God gives me the armor to withstand, if I choose.

I will, with all my being, choose Him.
You will not be my number one.
But because of this,
I will love you with a love that is more than feelings.

I will love you with everything He has shown me
on how to love.

My love will be a verb.

I will not be a number or a story for you to tell later in passing,
or a distant memory of times that will become only that.
I want to talk about these difficult times and hold tight the fight
together.

I will not give pieces of my soul to people
anymore than I already have.

Not until they say "forever"
and I believe them; then we will share our names,
And say "Goodnight."

Choice

I don't want to fall.
I want to walk into love.

Falling gives the sense of no choice.

I choose for it to be redeeming.
C.S. Lewis said,
"The only place that love does not exist is in hell."

But I want to represent God's love.
In order to do that, I must choose to walk into chances that
cause me to love.

To show love.
Love means to be vulnerable.
And that's okay.

letters

TO

Midnight
Moon

Midnight Moon

Midnight moon,
It's me again. Still unable to sleep.
The time of night when I ask all the questions
that cause my mind to not transition to dreams.
I try to do what others do, but I don't like counting sheep;
instead, I gaze at the stars that surround you and
connect the dots to make an outline of my favorite letters.
I love how they all shine bright together;
giving me just enough light to not be afraid.

Midnight moon,
I think of how you must envy the sun so much
of it's luminesce that you become hungry
and engulf its light each night to prepare us for its day.

Midnight moon,
My sweet friend. You calm my soul with your silence.
Hide my secrets in your dust and bury them well.
And midnight moon, just one more thing before I go;
If I could ask you just one more question.
A question I have hidden in the depths of my heart that only
comes out at night to cloud the sky, but a question that
always lingers until morning,
"What makes anyone stay?"

Fireflies

I saw fireflies tonight.
California doesn't have those.
They are such magical little creatures.

When I saw them, my face lit up.
When I was on the west coast, I remember thinking how I
missed seeing them.
And at that moment,
I was reminded that I no longer have to wake up scared.
Unaware how this body was going to be used.
And how I can now see fireflies light up the night.

False Promises

Don't believe the boy when he promises you the moon
when it was never his to give.

To Remember No More

Morbid thoughts at midnight.
They swirl through my mind
like the cotton white of fluffy sheep.
Thoughts of the next few years
of conversations that I cannot talk my way out of
pretending that what needs to be said cannot be.

We all have a choice.

But the last conversation. The last few years.
If you decide not to follow the path that leads to light,
will you have comfort in knowing that someone who was
formed in you is clothed in white?
Never afraid to sing and never filled with tears again?

I can't take this.

I don't know what to do.

Watching the bones wilt, the skin sag,
the hair turn dry and brittle,
reminds me that this vessel won't last.

We are not made for here.

I have heard that true followers
can be some of the most grievous of souls—

God letting me know that no tears will be shed there,
comforts me here.
But for now, I'm not there,
and I have collected too many jars of salted rain.

These things you will never know. These things I must hold.
These things, one day, I will let go and remember no more.

Late Night Walks

As I look up and connect the dots in the dark,
I breathe a refreshing scent of NEW.
I can use all my senses as I return
from wherever it was I went.
This is the year of "me"—
This is the year that I say, "no" and love it.
No apologies for being me.
Just me.

The Moon

It hides my secrets in its dust.
The moon is like me in that it isn't the light,
but a reflection of something much greater.

It has holes and patches,
but always shines regardless of its hurt.
Always giving and never asking for anything in return.

The moon is my friend, although he never asked to be.
Still, I wait for his shine to tuck me in to say "goodnight."

A.D.D.

I want to think of someone when the world is asleep.
The night sky, with the moon all aglow—
I'm too tired to weep.

Just random words to jot down
on this yellow pad with black ink.
"Man, this pen writes good."
Mind scattered—don't know what to think.

I am out of ideas for poems that deal with the hope,
the happiness, and the wantings of love.
Honestly, at this moment, I feel apathy,
because it will never fit me like a glove.

Random, oh random, pretty words that I write.
Words that make no sense as I turn out the light.

Good Morning Sunshine, Good Night Moonlight

Good morning sunshine.
As the light of the day shines upon my face through the
curtains of my eyelids,
I thank my God for another day.

I rise with curiosity of what your light will reveal to me today.

Great wonders and expectations of a day
beginning with no regret;
Full of promise and possibilities.

As you slowly fade to come back another day,
As I see your emblazed light over the horizon say farewell—
you graciously give your reflection to the night.

The glow shines radiantly upon the darkness as I wish upon
the stars that surround the moon.

My wishes swiftly shoot to a whisper in the illuminated sky.

It is getting late, so I pull the warmth of my blanket over me.
I thank my God for the adventures of the day and say,
"Goodnight moonlight. Never fade away."

"When I consider Your heavens,
The work of Your fingers,
The moon and the stars,
Which You ordained.
What is man that You are mindful of him,
And the son of man that You visit him?"
Psalm 8:3-4 NKJV

If this sounds like your story...

Family Care Homes
205-945-0037 | www.pathwaysprofessional.org

Raiin – National Sexual Assault Hotline
800-656-HOPE(4673) | www.raiin.org

The National Domestic Violence Hotline
1-800-799-SAFE (7233) | www.thehotline.org

Disaster Distress Helpline (24/7 Hotline)
1-800-5990

Gifts from Within (For survivors of trauma and victimization)
207-236-8858

Just One More Thing

P.S. Why do we fight to stay in a world where we don't belong?

P.P.S. Be as cruel as you want; it only makes my writing better.

P.P.P.S. I don't want people in my life that only stick around for the pretties.

P.P.P.P.S. Time does not take away the wrong,
    If it hasn't been made right.

P.P.P.P.P.S. One thing I have learned and feared:
    That people always leave.

P.P.P.P.P.P.S. I still want a fairytale, even if fairytales don't exist.

P.P.P.P.P.P.P.S. I am going to start calling it,
    "When I live" rather than "When I die."

P.P.P.P.P.P.P.P.S. Poems aren't always meant to be happy;
    it's just poor man's therapy.

P.P.P.P.P.P.P.P.P.S. Bitterness and pride are such easy pills to swallow
    and too easy to get addicted to, but like all pain killers,
    it will eventually become a part of who you are if you let it.

P.P.P.P.P.P.P.P.P.P.S. Sometimes I think half of my life is spent in frustration
    of being misunderstood.

P.P.P.P.P.P.P.P.P.P.P.S. "They act like I'm a sojourner or something."

Lisa Ann is a lover of words, Birmingham, and DIY crafts. When she is not working her full-time and two part-time side hustles, you can find her on Etsy making perfectly imperfect wood art for her shop *Lion and Lace Designs*.

Lisa proves it is never too late to be what you want to be when you grow up as she is pursuing a Bachelor's Degree in education, with a bucket list dream of being on the TEDx Birmingham stage.

Lisa's poetry and art have been featured by Button Poetry's social feeds. And while she never considered herself a spoken word poet, you can catch her from time to time behind the mic in Birmingham at local open mic nights.

⊙ thedramaticflower

About the Illustrator:

Melissa Shultz-Jones loves illustrating, especially for children. Her debut picture book came out in 2017, collecting fantastic reviews for her illustrations and a Moonbeam Award in Silver. Her happy place is hanging out with her husband and children. Dungeons and Dragons, board games, house shoes, and meandering conversations over coffee are her love languages.

To find out more about her work,
please visit melissashultz-jones.com.

List of poems in this publication originally printed in
The Stereotypical, Dramatic Life Of A Flower © 2015

The Little Girl On The Brick Wall

Marriage Is...

Satisfying The Unsatisfied

Thoughts From Aisle 7

I Always Knew

100% Cotton

The Ex Files

Counting It All As Joy

My Cup Overflows

The Love Letter: Part 1

Until Now

A Friendly Reminder

The Love Letter: Part II

The Return

Realization

Cleansing The Soul

The Ripple Effect

My Kind Of Love

New Words

Longing

Lisa's Song

Even Still

Choice

A.D.D.

Good Morning Sunshine, Good Night Moonlight

The End

Behind every "I don't know if I have it in me," there was God. He was leading me, telling me that He had me. With that being said, I will always thank God who is my all, and for every Romans 8:28 moment that intertwined the good with the bad. Thank you for being the God who goes before me, and giving me not only life, but a life with purpose.

He also gave me a few people along the way, that I would like to show appreciation to:

- My favorite Katie, my sister soul mate. I will continue to always say, "I don't think I could do life without you."
- To my boots-wearing friend, Rhett.
- And Loida, my forever friend. I know without a doubt that God put us in each other's lives at the exact perfect moment.
- My vintage friend, Dude—who is never too cool for greasy pizza and drive-by hugs
- My pup, Grace, and her grandmother, Denise.
- Button Poetry for the twenty playlists on my YouTube account.
- I thank Birmingham, my city, for allowing me the platform to share my words and listen.
- To all my spiritual family, friends, and Italian family who have supported me, loved me, laughed with me, cried with me, and have simply done life with me. Thank you. I love you all...
  agape and phileo style.